AUTOIMMUNE DISEASE

The Clean Eating Cookbook

My Road Back to Health...

Gluten, Dairy, Egg, Grain, Soy & Nut (not coconut) Free!!

Lisa Poloniato Marchese, CHN

FOREWORD BY Dr. Carissa Doherty, ND

Copyright © 2013 by Lisa Poloniato Marchese, CHN

ISBN 978-0-7414-8366-9 Black and White Paperback
ISBN 978-0-7414-8301-0 Color Paperback

Printed in the United States of America

Published April 2013

INFINITY PUBLISHING
1094 New DeHaven Street, Suite 100
West Conshohocken, PA 19428-2713
Toll-free (877) BUY BOOK
Local Phone (610) 941-9999
Fax (610) 941-9959
Info@buybooksontheweb.com
www.buybooksontheweb.com

DISCLAIMER

This is my story and what has worked for me.

All information and material in this book is for informational purposes only.

The information, thoughts and opinions in this book are solely mine.

They are not intended to replace or substitute that of your medical professional or health care provider.

If you have health issues or think something could be wrong always seek medical attention immediately.

As always, consult with your doctor before beginning any new diet, treatment or lifestyle plan.

If you have allergies or sensitivities to any foods or their by-product

mentioned in this book please do not consume.

CONTENTS

FOREWORD

I met Lisa several years ago and was immediately struck by her determination. Lisa had come to me to find out why she was experiencing several health issues. We discussed possible reasons and devised a plan. She committed her whole heart to changing her life and has never looked back. Using her body and mind as a guide, she pushed to know more about her health. Her goal was to achieve optimal health and she knew her body would tell her when she had found it. Lisa figured out very soon that a change in diet would result in dramatic health changes.

I remember Lisa telling me she loved the learning that had come with her health journey, but had wished someone had written down all the facts and tips that had taken her months and years to discover. I am thrilled that Lisa is now writing down all those golden nuggets of knowledge to help those who need a resource in their journey that will help change their lives, and in some cases save their lives.

In my practice as a naturopathic doctor, I need every person I see to change their diet in order to transform their health. I can't wait to tell them of Lisa's book so their process is much easier. Lisa's book is a wonderful resource for people who are committed to optimizing their health.

I specialize in women's health, fertility and dementia and my sister, Dr. Sonya Doherty specializes in autism. We have rarely seen a patient where diet change was not hugely life changing. Such changes include couples being able to conceive, the immune system being strengthened or children on the autism spectrum beginning to talk.

Every time I saw Lisa, she was energized and full of a thirst for knowledge. She was always sharing her knowledge and support with friends, family and other travelers on the road to wellness who benefited from her passion to stick to a healthy diet.

Lisa is dedicated to providing a resource with the details necessary to comply with an ancient concept of health from Hippocrates.

"Let food be thy medicine and medicine be thy food"

I hope her story and her amazing insight to detail help others on their journey to health.

Dr. Carissa Doherty ND

Naturopathic Doctor

www.naturalcareclinic.ca

Page of Love

I have been blessed with support from so many people from the beginning of my journey to where I am today.

Mom, you are my rock and inspiration. You taught me to never give up and to fight for what you want; I admire your strength and drive, I love you...xo

Dad, even though you are no longer with me on this earth, I know you are by my side holding my hand, guiding and loving me...xo

Richard and Lily, you make me proud every day, make me laugh so hard I cry and show me I am never too old to learn. Thank you both for all the taste testing you did, especially when things looked nothing like they were supposed to!! Lily for all the notes you took as I shouted changes from across the kitchen and Richard for your great photography...xo

Rich, even when you did not understand what I was going through you agreed to learn and have an open mind. Thank you for supporting my dreams, I am forever grateful...xo

Last but surely not least, my friends who listened to me for endless hours when I was in the depth of my pain, and offered their unconditional love and support. I can't even begin to thank you. Doreen, Sharon and Dr. K sending a special hug your way...xo

My Love Affair with the Kitchen....

There is nothing I love more than cooking, it has always been and always will be a passion of mine. I am by no means a trained culinary chef; I just go by what I have learned and follow my passions. As a young child I remember watching my parents cooking together in the kitchen and I relished how smoothly they moved around the fridge and stove like Olympic figure skaters gliding on the ice. When I had to adjust my diet, it all became so overwhelming, that I initially lost my passion for cooking. But as time went on, I knew I had to reignite that passion for both me, my family, and in honor of my parents!!

One little secret I will share is that as much as I love to cook, I am a lazy cook. I love all food, the aroma and textures as you create the recipes, the smells as they are cooking, and of course eating the finished product. But I am a mom of 2 active kids, run a house, deal with unreliable autoimmune issues, run a business and most of all like to get out and live life. Spending hours in the kitchen was not and is not an option for me. To solve this problem I found a little cookware product I LOVE, you know it as the food processor....I know it as my secret love affair with a kitchen appliance (it does not have to be a big fancy expensive one; I created this whole cookbook with a small hand sized processor that cost me $20).

Most if not every recipe in this cookbook is made with a simple flick of the food processor button. Toss all the ingredients in, hit start, that's it. Now I will occasionally ask you to pull out the stove top grill, or sauce pan, but I definitely don't ask you to separate the wet and the dry, mix, add together, then incorporate here and there. Nope not in this book, this is the lazy man's cookbook; just toss everything in one bowl, mix, and go!!!

Substitutions

Meat dishes can be substituted for other meats. If a recipe calls for beef feel free to replace it with chicken, turkey, pork or fish. If you have an issue with coconut milk but not nuts or seeds, replace the coconut milk with a nut or seed milk unless it calls for canned coconut milk, as it is a thicker version of regular coconut milk. If you want to make **homemade coconut milk for the recipes that don't call for canned, simply blend 1 cup shredded unsweetened coconut with 1.5 cups water in a high speed blender and puree (no need to strain the milk).**

Sugar is Sugar even in its natural state

I try to use dates as a sweetener as much as possible, but there are times when you just need that extra kick. When I mention dates as an ingredient, I am speaking of something called a medjool date. They are bigger and softer than regular dates. If you can't find them, no worries regular dates will work, you just might want to add an extra date or two to get the same sweetness.

The occasional recipe calls for honey or pure maple syrup (and I think two recipes have chocolate). These recipes are intended as occasional foods; excessive sugar in any form is not good for our immune system or our body in general.

Other Fun Facts

To make a recipe from the main meal section a complete meal, add a large side salad, steamed greens, veggies of your choice or one of the side dishes from this book. Another fun thing about all my recipes...they can be eaten raw. That's right, since there is no egg or grain, except for the animal protein, most dishes do not need to be cooked, and let me tell you, some tasted better raw. But I will leave that up to you!!

Most ingredients can be found at your local supermarket or health food store. I made each recipe as simple, fast and easy as I could, so whether you are a mom on the go, or dealing with autoimmune fatigue, you can still get a nice meal on the table for your family.

I hope you enjoy eating and creating the recipes as much as my family and I did..... Much joy, Lisa....xo

The Look of Autoimmune Disease

"The best way to teach is by telling a story"- Kenneth H Blanchard

If you are reading this book chances are you or someone you know is dealing with an autoimmune disease.

Whatever you are feeling I have been there, I understand. I wanted to write this book to share my story and what worked for me. In my opinion you can feel better, you are not alone, and you can regain your energy, and get your life back. How do I know, because I did it!!

When my journey with autoimmune issues started years back, I felt very alone. It felt like there was nowhere to turn, no one seemed to understand, and even though my mom, husband, children and a handful of friends really tried, I still felt very isolated and I don't want that for you. It is important that you know whatever you are feeling, it is your truth and it is valid!!

Autoimmune sufferers all have very different stories, yet in so many ways our stories are almost the same, you knew something was wrong, you just felt off. You became more tired than normal, achy; you never completely bounced back from that cold or bout with the flu. Maybe after child birth things did not seem right, or it could have been as simple as feeling fine one day, only to wake up the next feeling like you had been hit by a Mac truck. Whatever the case, you basically felt like "What the hell just happened to me". The fatigue, overwhelming nausea, migraines, vision issues, anxiety, depression, muscle and joint pain, bloating, skin issues, playing with your kids, socializing with friends, even walking to the bathroom all become too much to bare. You sit and wonder how life's pleasures now became the most exhausting things ever. It's like your world is spinning out of control, every noise sounds like someone is screaming in your ear and every word is like nails on a chalk board.

Then there are the thoughts and opinions of the outside world. Family, friends, doctors, specialist, coworkers, you can see it in their eyes; they think you have become a hypochondriac or maybe just desperate for attention. Remember, you look fine on the outside.

I think one of the biggest hurdles autoimmune sufferers face is that most (not all) autoimmune disease is not visible to the outside world. People see you, you look the same, talk the same, maybe even act the same, but on the inside you feel nowhere close to the person you used to be. I like to call this the lipstick face, as long as you look good on the outside, the lipstick is on, and the smile is there, then all must be fine….Yet behind the lipstick lies your truth….all those symptoms no one can see.

"Don't let the noise of others drown your own inner voice" – Steve Jobs

You Are NOT Alone
Where Have You Been & Where Are You Going…

How did this road start for me, I had come down with pneumonia but I never bounced back, I never felt like the same person. I knew something else was wrong but I didn't know what. I went from being an energetic active woman, running errands, volunteering at school; working as a special education teaching assistant, jogging 3 miles a day, working part time at my local library and my most important job, being a mom to two fabulous kids. To barely being able to walk from one room to the next without assistance, all within a matter of days.

I would later learn that my bout with pneumonia had kicked in years of undiagnosed Hashimoto, Celiac and Raynaud's. On top of all that, I went from being a creative, passionate cook, to fearing all foods, even rice; yes even rice seemed to make me feel ill. All I knew was most foods were making me feel sick.

Most autoimmune sufferers don't even know what is wrong at first; we think the worst, feel like we are dying, our body keeps shifting and changing and we just want answers. The problem is it usually takes many years of suffering and testing for an autoimmune disease to finally get diagnosed.

All sorts of symptoms began flooding my life and became what I knew as my new normal. After visiting numerous doctors, specialists, alternative and naturopathic doctors, tons of blood work, ultrasounds, x-rays, and MRI's, I was thrilled to find out nothing serious was wrong. But then what was wrong? Why was my body shutting down right before my eyes? What was it trying to tell me? And why could I not understand it?

I would sit for hours searching the internet, reading hundreds and hundreds of books, I tried every diet and supplement out there but nothing was working. I could feel the anxiety rising in me with every passing moment yet I still had no answers, I felt like I was fighting for my life and the clock was ticking….

Through all the initial testing, I did find out I was B12, vitamin D deficient (very common in autoimmune sufferers) and gluten intolerant. Supplementation seemed to help the vitamin deficiencies, as well as riding the tingling in my hands and feet (a sign of B12 deficient). The gluten intolerance explained the IBS, vitamin deficiencies, and why I was suddenly struggling with so many food sensitivities and anxiety (yes, anxiety is a gluten intolerant/celiac symptom) check, check and check, we were getting closer. I was told there was not much that could be done other than to start a gluten free diet and I should feel better. I was thrilled I had an answer, I had struck gold and I could now get my life back!!

Problem was I was not feeling better, in fact not long after starting the gluten free diet I actually began to feel worse. The bloating got so bad I could barely breath, IBS through the roof, migraines became part of my daily routine, the muscle inflammation and joint pain was at its worst, the overall fatigue was so bad, that even going from room to room was once again almost impossible. Something was still wrong; through all of this my husband, children and I relocated to another country.

When we got settled I had another bout with a swollen thyroid and my fingers where once again turning white. I went to see my new doctor and showed him what had been happening all those years. He took one look at me and said I think you have thyroid issues and Raynaud's phenomenon. He ran a bunch of tests, and called me a few days later, to say "you have Hashimoto disease"….Hashi what? And you carry the genetic gene for Celiac disease.

Since I had been playing around with a gluten-free diet for years, my blood test for Celiac disease kept coming back inconclusive and a biopsy would not have been accurate unless I decided to do a gluten challenge (eating full on gluten containing foods for minimum 3-6 week). After much discussion with my doctor and a specialist in the celiac field, I decided not to return to a gluten induced diet. I knew how I felt, I carried the gene, it was in my family history and my doctor and I felt good about my decision.

As for Hashimoto disease, it is an autoimmune issue that can throw your thyroid off and make it fluctuate back and forth from hyper to hypothyroidism (some with Hashimoto have no symptoms) which explained the weight loss and weight gain I had been experiencing. I had lost and gained the same 25lbs within a matter of months. Side note, Hashimoto and Celiac/gluten Intolerance seem to be showing up more often hand in hand, so if you know you have one ask to be checked for the other.

Now I sat in peace, give me some meds and I would feel better. Well not in my case, all my other thyroid numbers were still in a very good range, which was a good thing, it meant that my thyroid was working hard to stay balanced and functioning well. However, since I had high antibody numbers this told my doctor it was an autoimmune issue; and would most likely in time burn out my thyroid (treating Hashimoto disease with medication when other thyroid numbers are in the normal range is a controversial subject and one that needs to be discussed between you and your doctor). I chose not to medicate, my doctor was supportive of my decision and was willing to work with me. So what was I to do? I was not about to give up this 6 year fight now. I knew having an autoimmune disease meant your immune system picked an organ to attack, in my case the thyroid was the main attraction. So I was back to needing to figure out how to strengthen my immune system.

"Someday everything will make perfect sense, it just might not be today" - Unknown

When Gluten Free Is Not the Answer

Now I confess when I started playing with a gluten free lifestyle years ago, I went from a diet that contained some standard American diet processed foods, to gluten free processed foods. Pizza, bread, donuts, brownies, cookies, no problem they were all available in a gluten free form, the transition was easy and my life did not have to change much. Maybe that was the problem; I was just switching regular junk food out for the gluten free version. My immune system was definitely not going to heal or rebuild itself that way; I had to figure something else out. Enter the world of what I like to call the clean eating autoimmune protocol but is better known as a paleolithic lifestyle. No grains, no dairy, no gluten, and no processed sugars. I had already been dairy-free for other reasons, so that was covered, but I was definitely going to struggle with the sugar thing; I was a self-proclaimed sugar addict. Hmm could this work? At this point I had nothing to lose except hopefully all of my horrid symptoms that were preventing me from living my life.

Let's be honest, it was without a doubt much easier to go from my regular lifestyle to a gluten-free lifestyle than from a gluten free lifestyle to what I was about to attempt!! Did you follow that?

After a few hours, ok more like a few days of crying and trying to figure out how to eat and not starve, (good bye PB & Jam). I was overwhelmed and out of control, I wanted to crawl into a hole and sulk. But that was not going to get me anywhere, the boots straps had to get pulled up once again.

"Hell there are no rules here – we're trying to accomplish something"- Thomas Edison

The Autoimmune Protocol

I began reading and learning all I could about a grain free, dairy free lifestyle. Problem was there were other so called healthy nutritious foods that seemed to bother me. Enter the autoimmune protocol.

Based on what I was feeling and noticing with certain foods, this style of eating made even more sense but would definitely be more challenging. Eggs had to be eliminated which was fine, eating them made me feel ill anyway, but how was I to bake without them? You also had to remove nightshades (potato, peppers, eggplant, tomato, and goji berries and their by-products) and nuts; the arthritis like discomfort I would feel in my knees and fingers from the nightshades was enough to say sayonara, and the nuts where not digesting well anyway, (even soaked or spouted).

Now, you are probably scratching your head thinking then what the heck am I supposed to eat, bake with, or oh ya, did I mention eat!!!

Not to worry that is where I come in.....that is why you have this book in your hand; I did all the work for you, I shed the tears for you, tossed out many disgusting flopped out recipes for you, and spent hours creating and recreating recipes just for YOU...Yes you read that right, you don't have to do a thing, just make the recipes, eat, and be happy!!

Where am I on my journey today you might wonder, well I am ecstatic to report I am still on no medication, my antibody numbers are all still sitting happily in the normal range, and I have not had a Raynaud's episode in over a year. I have a great team of doctors that I work with that consist of both western and alternative medicine, who make sure my tests stay in the normal range and that I stay balanced and on track.

I went back to school and graduated Holistic Nutrition, and through it all I started a Facebook page that is filled with fun loving wonderful people just like you. I also launched a website full of great info and more recipes, so pop over, check us out and say hi www.autoimmuneandyou.com

So as you can see I have gotten my life back, feel energized and I want the same for you!!.....xo

"Clean Eating is like skinny dipping...
You strip everything down to its natural state and dive right in" – Me

Amazing Appetizers, Dips & Side Dishes

Pizza Cups

We love Hawaiian pizza, so we thought how fun to have a grab and go version!!

Preheat oven 425° F

Serves 6

2 cups pineapple, chopped

2 cups mushrooms, chopped

2 cups green onions, chopped

Sea salt, dash

12 thin slices of ham (or deli meat)

1. Place first 4 ingredients in mixing bowl and mix together.
2. Place one piece of ham into a 12 serving muffin tin and bake for 20 minutes.
3. Let ham cups cool, and fill with pineapple mixture.

Nachos

Yum....Nachos, I love nachos,

In fact one of my favorite past times was to go to a well-known little cheesecake location and order a big ol' plate!!

A grain and dairy free version was definitely a must...

Preheat oven 350° F

Serves 4

4 sweet potatoes

2 avocados

1 small can black olives

½ cup pineapple, sliced

1 tbsp. cilantro

Sea salt, dash

1/2 a lime, juiced

1. Slice potatoes into thin chip like pieces.
2. Place on parchment lined baking sheet, bake 20-25 minutes or until cooked and golden brown.
3. In mixing bowl add flesh of the 2 avocados, lime juice, sea salt, and cilantro and mash all together.
4. Take sweet potato chips and top with guacamole, pineapple, and olives.

You can make this a complete meal by topping the nachos with your favorite ground or diced meat.

Grilled Scallops

Have your guests thinking you took a gourmet cooking class or two.

This super easy, yet fancy looking appetizer is sure to please!!

Serves 4

16 large scallops

2 tbsp. olive oil

Topping

1/3 cup balsamic vinegar

3 tbsp. maple syrup

2 cloves garlic

2 tbsp. bacon bits

1. Drizzle scallops with olive oil.
2. Grill on stove top grill until cooked through.
3. In sauce pan, mix vinegar and maple syrup, bring to a boil and remove from heat.
4. Top scallops with vinegar mixture, pureed garlic and bacon bits.

*Make this a complete meal by making a huge salad or steamed greens and topping the greens with 4-6 scallops per person.

Sushi Rolls

My son loves sushi; in fact I think if I let him he would live off of it.

But with all the rice and wheat ingredients that can be found in them, we came up with this tasty grain free alternative....

Serves 4-6 as an appetizer

Serves 2 as a main meal

4 nori wraps

4 pieces of beef, thinly sliced

1 tbsp. olive oil

1 tbsp. balsamic vinegar

1. Grill the beef strips to your desired liking.
2. Place in the wrap and fill with topping of your choice. We used cucumber, avocado and carrots in ours.
3. Wrap into a sushi roll and drizzle with olive oil and vinegar.
4. Slice into small bite sized pieces and enjoy!!

*To make this a main meal, cut each roll in half, and serve with a nice big side salad, or steamed veggies and homemade Sweet Potato Chips (see Nacho recipe).

Cabbage Salad

This salad can be eaten warm or cold.

Perfect for a nice summer BBQ, or a pleasant side dish in the cold of winter.

Serves 4-6

1 large bag shredded cabbage (raw or cooked)

1 cup blueberries (fresh)

½ tsp. ground ginger

½ lemon, juiced

1 cup pineapple juice

1 cup grapes, sliced in half

1 grapefruit, sectioned and diced

3 green onions, chopped

Sea salt, dash

1. Toss cabbage raw or cooked into a large bowl.
2. In food processor add blueberries, ginger, lemon juice, and pineapple juice and puree.
3. Pour dressing over cabbage and toss.
4. Add in grapes, grapefruit and onions.
5. Serve and enjoy!!

*Feel free to build this up and make it a complete meal by adding ground turkey or a nice side of grilled fish.

Bacon Pineapple Wraps

I owe this one to my friend Laurie!!

She served it at her 4th of July party and I became addicted immediately!!

Preheat oven 425° F

Serves 4-6

12 strips of bacon

1 pineapple, fresh peeled and cored

1. Slice the pineapple into 2-3 inch long pieces.
2. Cut the bacon strips in half.
3. Wrap one piece of bacon around 1 piece of pineapple. Continue this process until all bacon pieces are used.
4. Place on baking sheet and bake until the bacon is to the crispness you adore….

*Substitute the pineapple with dates, peaches, asparagus or pears.

Coconut Shrimp

Nothing reminds me of the tropics more than a Pina Colada, and some nice cold shrimp. I thought I would bring a little of the tropics to NY.

Serves 6

12 jumbo shrimp

1 tbsp. coconut oil

2 cloves garlic, finely chopped

½ orange, juiced

1 tbsp. raw honey

¼ cup shredded coconut

1. In wok or stove top pan heat oil, garlic and shrimp 15 minutes or until shrimp turns pink and fully cooked.
2. Add in orange juice, honey and shredded coconut.
3. Toss and serve.

*To make this a complete meal, place 6-8 shrimp over a large plate of raw or steamed greens of choice.

Herb Crackers

If you ever take the time to read the labels on most cracker boxes, you will notice they have everything in them but cracker stuff....Oh boy, what were my taste buds to do!!

Preheat oven 300° F

Makes approximately 20 crackers

1/3 cup coconut oil (melted)

1/3 tsp. baking powder

1/4 cup water

1 tbsp. olive oil

1/3 cup coconut flour

1 tsp. dried parsley

1 tsp. dried chives

1 tsp. dried onion

Sea salt, dash or 2

1. Mix first 4 ingredients with hand mixer in large bowl.
2. Slowly add in flour until all mixed.
3. Add in herbs and mix by hand and roll into ball.
4. Line baking sheet with parchment paper and put dough on it.
5. Place another piece of paper over top and with rolling pin roll out into a thin layer.
6. Using a knife, score dough into cracker shapes.
7. Top with a little sprinkle of sea salt.
8. Bake 8-15 minutes or until golden brown.
9. Let cool and separate into cracker pieces.

*Make sure to keep a close eye, they cook quickly and you don't want them to burn. Also make sure the dough is rolled out as even as possible or they will burn on the edges and not fully cook in the middle.
*These crackers get crunchier and tastier the longer you leave them out. So this is a case where day old is best!!

Sweet Potato Chips

No need putting the napkins out for this one
I guarantee your guests will want to lick their fingers clean!!!

Preheat oven 350° F

Serves 4

2 large sweet potatoes

2-3 tbsp. coconut oil

2 tbsp. cinnamon

2-3 tbsp. maple syrup

1. Thinly slice your potatoes and place on parchment lined baking sheet, bake 20-30 minutes or until cooked through and golden brown.
2. Heat coconut oil in frying pan and add in potatoes from the oven and fry up until golden brown.
3. Remove from heat and put in a big bowl, toss with maple syrup and cinnamon.
4. Put on a plate and let cool......

*Add these quick and easy delicious chips to any dip from the dip section of the book.

Stuffed Mushrooms

I have never been a big fan of mushrooms, but when they are cooked to perfection like these and stuffed with all this goodness not even I could resist....

Preheat oven 350° F

Serves 2-3

1 cup celery, chopped

1 cup green onions, chopped

1/3 cup raisins

3 large carrots, shredded

3 tbsp. olive oil

6 large mushrooms, cleaned and stemmed

1. Toss first 5 ingredients in a pan and sauté until the celery is cooked through.
2. If you need to add a little water along the way to help it steam feel free, but just in small amounts. Also stir constantly to prevent burning.
3. Put mushrooms in small oven pan and drizzle with olive oil, bake 20 minutes or until tender and golden brown.
4. Stuff mushrooms with filling and enjoy...

*These are great appetizers to any party or get together. But you can also turn them into a quick and easy main course by adding any type of ground meat or diced chicken to the mix to make them a complete meal.

Grilled Zucchini with Maple Dip

The mix of the sweet from the dip and the salty from the zucchini is a fun combo

Preheat stove top grill

Serves 6-8

4 zucchinis

2-3 tbsp. olive oil

Sea salt, dash

DIP

¼ tsp. turmeric

½ tsp. onion flakes

½ tsp. dill

¼ cup canned coconut milk

1 tbsp. maple syrup

1. Slice zucchini into 1" pieces and drizzle with olive oil.
2. Grill on low heat until cooked on both sides.
3. Whisk turmeric, onion, maple syrup and coconut milk together.
4. Put on plate and serve.

Garlic Ginger Crackers

These are a fun cracker they have a sweet yet warming flavor to them from the ginger.
They make a great accompaniment to the chicken noodle soup, or broccoli curry in this book.

Preheat oven 350° F

Makes 8 large or 12 small

1/3 cup coconut flour

¼ cup water

1/3 cup coconut oil (melted)

½ tsp. cinnamon

¼ cup maple syrup

1 tsp. lemon juice

½ tsp. garlic powder

½ tsp. ginger powder

½ tsp. sage (optional)

1 tsp. parsley

½ tsp. turmeric

½ tsp. cinnamon

1 tsp. onion powder

1. Mix everything in large bowl until it forms dough.
2. Take small pieces of dough and roll into balls and flatten out with your hands.
3. Place on parchment lined baking sheet.
4. Bake approximately 20 minutes or until golden brown.

*Add to any of the dips or spreads, or as a crunchy treat with a nice big salad or bowl of soup.

Kale Chips

Who needs popcorn!!

Your guests will love munching on these while watching football or a good movie.

Simple, quick, tasty and easy to make!!

Preheat oven 350° F

Serves 2

1 head kale

1 tbsp. olive oil

1 tbsp. dried onion flakes (optional)

1 tbsp. garlic powder (optional)

Sea salt, dash

1. Wash and chop or tear kale into med size pieces (they will shrink when they bake).
2. Toss kale into a bowl and drizzle with olive oil and sea salt.
3. Massage the oil into the kale.
4. Spread out on a parchment lined baking sheet.
5. Bake 15-20 minutes or until crispy.
6. Scoop into bowl, (if you choose to add the garlic and onion now is the time) grab the movie, kick back and ENJOY...

*Keep an eye out, they can burn easy!! Speaking from experience ;)
*If you still eat nuts you can make these into cheesy flavored chips by tossing some grated brazil nuts over top once they are cooked.
*These will disappear fast so I suggested making double the batch.
*The chips will shrink down once baked.

Tropical Brussel Sprouts

I added a tropical twist to what seems to be the comeback veggie of the year
The brussel sprout!!
Serve them in fancy little individual cups as appetizers
or make them a nice side dish to any main meal...

Preheat oven 350° F

Serves 4-6 (as a side dish)

1 large bag brussel sprouts (approximately 30 sprouts)

2 yellow zucchinis

1 red apple

1 can or fresh pineapple

½ cup raisins

1/2 cup shredded carrot

1. Bake brussel sprouts in glass baking pan filled with about 3-4 inches of water for 70–90 minutes or until tender.
2. Chop raw zucchini, apple and pineapple into diced pieces.
3. Mix sprouts and all other ingredients together, drizzle with olive oil, balsamic vinegar and a dash of sea salt.
4. Serve.

*Brussel sprouts are yummy cooked or raw. If you have thyroid issues I suggest you always eat them cooked or steamed.
*To make this beautiful looking dish a complete meal, add it to a protein of your choice.

Asparagus Salad

You can enjoy this salad warm or cold.
It is nice as a warm side dish to steak or chicken.
Yet nice chilled with grilled fish or pureed into a chilled soup.

Serves 2

1 large bunch fresh asparagus

1 pear

1 large beet, peeled and chopped

2 tbsp. olive oil

1 tbsp. balsamic vinegar

Sea salt, dash

1. Steam asparagus until tender.

2. Spiral pear with a veggie spiral machine.

3. Put pear in bowl and top with asparagus and chopped beet.

4. Drizzle with olive oil, vinegar and dash of salt.

5. Serve.

*If using as a chilled soup once asparagus is steamed, toss all ingredients (except olive oil and vinegar) into a food processor or high speed blender and puree until creamy.

Coconoda dip

This is a new twist on an old time favorite…. Guacamole!!
Or a fabulous replacement for mayo on any "sandwich"

Serves 4-6

1/2 cup canned coconut milk

1 avocado

2 tbsp. fresh basil

2 cloves garlic

1 tbsp. dried onion flakes

1. Toss all ingredients into blender and puree until smooth.
2. Serve with a nice array of fresh chopped veggies, as a creamy salad dressing or to top your favorite steamed greens.

*Serve with the Herb Crackers, fresh veggies, or as a mayo style dressing on any sandwich.

Olive dip

This creation came one day when I was craving creamy ranch dressing

Serves 4-6

1 soft avocado

8-10 black or green pitted olives

1 clove garlic

Sea salt, pinch

1 lime, juiced

1. Put everything in a food processor and blend until creamy smooth.
2. If it's too thick add a little water a bit at a time until it's the consistency you like.

*Serve with chopped veggies, or the Sweet Potato Chips from the Nacho recipe.
*Turn this into a ranch style dressing by adding more water (a little at a time) to make it thin enough to pour over salad.

Cauliflower Tahini

I love the flavors of Greek food, so a dairy free replacement for tahini was a must.

Serves 6

1 head cauliflower

1 tsp. dill

3 cloves garlic

3 tsp. olive oil

1 tbsp. coconut milk

1. Cook the cauliflower until soft.
2. Toss everything into a food processor and puree until smooth.
3. Serve with chopped veggies, as a spread on sandwiches or as a topping to the nachos or potato skins.

*This is very spicy from all the garlic so adjust to your liking.

Maple Dip

This dip has both a sweet, yet salty taste all mixed into one...
Serve with the Herb Crackers from this book, or fresh veggies.

Makes 1 large bowl

¼ tsp. turmeric

½ tsp. onion flakes

½ tsp. dill

¼ tsp. sea salt

¼ cup canned coconut milk

1 tbsp. maple syrup

1. Put everything into a large bowl and whisk together.

2. Serve

Olive Oil "Butter" Spread

As a kid I loved the garlic bread my family would make.

My parents owned a bakery, so my dad would bring a fresh baked French loaf home and my mom would whip up some yummy garlic spread to top it off....

Well since the dairy is gone as is the bread, I needed to improvise as some old time favorites are not meant to die

1/4 cup olive oil

3-4 cloves of garlic or to your taste

Sea salt, dash

1. Puree all together until smooth.
2. Pour into container and freeze.

*Use as a butter on the Herb Crackers recipe, as a sauce mixed into a veggie dish, or pour over grilled or baked fish.
*For a dip use right away, for butter like spread, take out from freezer and let sit out to soften up and then use....

Turnip Fries

My kids and I love French fries, it's just that simple.

But I definitely don't want all of those chemicals in the store bought frozen kind going into our bodies...

The problem needed to be fixed, and fast!!

Preheat oven 425° F

Serves 2

1 turnip

1 tbsp. coconut flour

2 tbsp. olive oil

1 tsp. onion flakes

Sea salt, dash or 2

1. Slice turnip into thick match stick style pieces.

2. Toss turnip pieces and olive oil in small bowl until fully covered.

3. Sprinkle with sea salt, coconut flour, and onion flakes and toss until all mixed.

4. Spread out on parchment lined baking sheet; bake 30 minutes or until golden brown.

5. These will not get crunchy like "fried" french fries unless you choose to fry them in oil...

*Gently turn fries over half way through the baking time.
*I put these under the side dish part of the book, but they definitely could also be used as an appetizer with a nice dipping sauce on the side.
*You can also use sweet potato, carrots or rutabaga in place of the turnip.

Broccoli Bacon Curry

What can I say about the amazing and flavorful taste of curry except YUM!!!
Oh and did you catch that it's mixed with a hint of bacon.....Double yum!

Serves 4

1 head broccoli

1 cup canned coconut milk

1 tbsp. turmeric

1 tsp. cinnamon

½ tsp. nutmeg

1 cup bacon bits

1. Steam head of broccoli and chop into bite size pieces.
2. Mix other 5 ingredients into a large bowl and add in broccoli, toss and serve.

*This can of course be upgraded to a lovely side dish by accompanying any of your favorite protein.

Magnificent Meals

Citrus Sole

This is a twist on one of my mom's classics.

Preheat oven 350° F

Serves 2

2 large pieces sole

1 large orange, juiced

1 large lemon, juiced

¼ cup olive oil

2 cloves garlic, pureed

1 tbsp. parsley, chopped.

1. Put fish in glass oven pan.

2. Mix lemon, orange juice, garlic and olive oil in bowl and pour over fish.

3. Sprinkle with chopped parsley and some sliced lemon and orange if you would like.

*You can also replace the fish with chicken or thinly sliced beef.

Dreamy Drumsticks

These are super easy and make great leftovers the next day.
Toss in the kid's lunch, or take chicken off the bone and add to a huge salad.

Preheat oven 425° F

Serves 4

8 chicken drumsticks

8 dates, (pitted and soaked)

½ cup coconut milk, canned

½ tsp. turmeric

½ tsp. rosemary

1 tsp. parsley

1 pear

½ cup olive oil

1. Puree everything in food processor except chicken and olive oil.

2. Put chicken in a glass oven pan.

3. Pour olive oil over chicken.

4. Top with puree.

5. Cover and bake 65 minutes or until chicken is golden brown and cooked through.

*Side with our Sweet Potato Chips, Broccoli Bacon Curry or Brussel Sprout recipe.

BLT Salad

Bacon Lettuce and tomato sandwiches are one of my family's favorites.
Here is a lettuceized (I know not a word) version...

Serves 2 as a meal

Serves 4 as a side salad

2 heads romaine lettuce

1 avocado

1 cup black olives, pitted

1 large package of bacon (cooked)

½ cup olive oil

¼ cup vinegar of choice

1. Wash lettuce and chop into bite size pieces.

2. Put everything into a large bowl and toss with oil and vinegar.

3. Place on two plates and top with equally divided pieces of bacon.

*This is a lite but filling meal. To make it more of a hearty feast feel free to top the salad with some grilled chicken or beef and then the bacon!!

Stuffed "Sweet" Potato Skins

Filled with all this goodness these make a great quick and easy meal.

Serves 4

2 sweet potatoes

1 package ground turkey

½ cup chopped chives + 1 tbsp.

½ cup bacon bits

1 tbsp. olive oil

1 clove garlic

1. Cook sweet potato and slice horizontally in half.
2. Scoop out the middle of the potato and reserve.
3. Toss potato reserve in food processor with 1 tbsp. olive oil, 1 clove of garlic and 1 tbsp. chives.
4. Puree until smooth.
5. In stove top pan cook up ground turkey and when cooked add in potato filling and mix together.
6. Scoop turkey mixture into sweet potato boats.
7. Top with remaining chives and bacon.

Cauliflower Tahini *for a sour cream like feel, add a scoop of Cauliflower Tahini

1 head cauliflower

1 tsp. dill

3 cloves garlic

3 tsp. olive oil

1 tbsp. coconut milk

1. Cook the cauliflower until soft.
2. Toss everything into a food processor and puree until smooth.

Salmon Bacon Wrap

Salmon is high in Omega 3 fats, can make your skin glow and your hair shine.
Since we have to eat it, why not wrap it in bacon!!

Preheat stove top grill

Preheat oven 350° F

Serves 4

4 salmon fillets (wild salmon if you can)

12 pieces of bacon

1. Grill the salmon until cooked through.

2. Take cooked salmon and wrap with 3 pieces of bacon.

3. Place on baking sheet and put in oven 15-20 minutes or until the bacon is the crispness you like.

*You can eat this as is or top it with the Mushroom Sauce (see below).
*A nice complimentary side dish would be a huge salad or the Asparagus Salad with pears.

Mushroom Sauce

6 mushrooms

4 tbsp. canned coconut milk

1 tsp. onion flakes

1 tsp. turmeric

Sea salt, dash

1. Toss all 5 ingredients into a food processor and blend until smooth.

2. Put sauce into a sauce pan and heat.

3. Pour evenly over cooked salmon.

Stuffed Artichokes

I LOVE stuffed artichokes, my mom always made them when I was kid.
The ones she made were filled with breadcrumbs and all kinds of other yumminess.
I did a little head scratching and came up with these gigantic bundles of love...

Serves 4

4 large artichokes

4 cans tuna

2 cans artichoke hearts

1/3 cup olive oil

2 cloves garlic

Sea salt, dash

1 tbsp. lemon zest

1 tbsp. parsley fresh or dried

½ cup shredded carrots

½ cup cooked bacon, finely chopped

1. Cut 1 inch off bottom of the artichokes and place in stove top pan with 5-6 inches water (enough to cover bottom half of the artichoke) cover and steam until very tender.
2. In a food processor puree tuna, canned artichokes, olive oil, garlic, sea salt.
3. Put mixture in bowl and add in lemon, parsley, carrots, and bacon and mix together by hand.
4. Fill artichokes with mixture.

*This is a fabulous meal all in one pretty little spot, but honestly I could have eaten two so you might want to make double!!

Citrus Chicken

Lemon chicken is a favorite to many when ordering Chinese food.
This rendition has a citrus twist and no wheat or soy!!

Serves 4-6

6 chicken breasts (bone in or deboned)

4 large oranges

4 cloves garlic

2 inch piece fresh ginger

1. Juice the oranges and put into food processor with garlic and ginger blend together.
2. Put chicken and orange juice mixture in a large bag and let marinate in the fridge for a few hours.
3. Pour everything into a stove top pan and cook until browned and cooked through.
4. Top with chopped green onions and orange zest.

*For a change feel free to give this a try with your favorite fish and a nice big salad, or steamed greens of your choice.

Sausage & Bok Choy

This meal could not be any faster for a night when a quick meal is needed;
Yet it looks so fancy the family will think you spent hours on it!!

Serves 4-6

8 sausages

8 baby bok choy

1 cup fresh orange juice

4 dates (soaked)

1 clove garlic

1. Grill sausage and place on top of baby bok choy.
2. Put orange juice, dates and garlic in food processor and blend until mixed.
3. Drizzle over bok choy and sausage and enjoy.

*You can also steam the bok choy, or fry it up with onions and other veggies you love.

Beef Chutney

Beef can get boring, so we added a punch of zing to this one to make your taste buds dance!!
This would be super yummy on pork as well.....

Serves 4

4 cuts of beef (your choice)

1 cup cherries

1 cup peaches

¼ tsp. nutmeg

½ tsp. crushed rosemary

1. Grill the beef.
2. Put cherries, peaches, nutmeg and fennel in a food processor and pulse to a chunky consistency.
3. Top over beef and serve.

*Want something lighter, use chicken, fish or pork instead.

Salmon Cakes

These hold together and bake up beautifully.

They are crunchy on the outside and moist and flaky on the inside.

Serves 2-3

Makes 6 large patties or 10 small

4 cups spinach, chopped

2 cups fresh salmon canned or fresh (if using fresh salmon, make sure it is precooked)

1 green onion

2 large sweet potatoes, precooked and peeled

1 tbsp. parsley

1/3 cup olive oil

½ lemon, juiced

1 small can black or green olives

1-2 heads of lettuce

2 tbsp. dijon mustard

1 lemon juiced

¾ cup olive oil

1. Put first 8 ingredients into a food processor and puree until smooth but a little chunky.
2. Form into round patties and place on parchment lined baking sheet.
3. Bake 30-40 minutes or until golden brown.
4. Wash and clean lettuce and chop into bite size pieces.
5. Whisk dijon mustard, 1 juiced lemon and the ¾ cup olive oil together and pour over lettuce.
6. Top with salmon cakes.

*Don't want to cook them!! No problem, shape into patties and serve raw.
*Mix thing up by replacing the salmon with tuna or finely chopped chicken.

Zucchini Fettuccine

Yum, a warm bowl of cream filled pasta, what could be better....
How about a nice warm bowl of cream filled pasta sans the grains, or dairy!!

Serves 4

4 large green zucchini

2 large yellow zucchini

½ cup canned coconut milk

½ lemon, juiced

½ tsp. onion flakes

1.5 tsp. maple syrup

1. Blend everything except the green zucchini in a food processor or high speed blender.

2. Make zucchini "pasta" with the green zucchini. The best way to do this is with a vegetable spiral maker.

3. Pour the "cream" sauce over the zucchini "pasta".

4. Toss and serve.

*This can be eaten as a cold salad, lovely for a picnic or family gathering. You can also warm it up and serve like a big ol' bowl of homemade fettuccini.
*Want something hardier, top with some ground beef, chicken, turkey or shrimp.

Chicken Italian Style

This recipe is in honor of my mom. Like most of my cooking and recipe ideas, they stem from my childhood favorites.

Whenever we had big family gatherings, this meal always made its way onto the table.

It is super easy and was always a big hit.

This one is for you mom!!

Preheat oven 350° F

Serves 6

6 large boneless chicken breasts

2 cans whole artichokes

1 large can black olives or fresh olives if you can find them

1 cup grapes

2 cup olive oil

1. Put all 4 ingredients in a large glass roasting pan, bake 45-60 minutes or until chicken is cooked fully.

2. That's it, it's that easy!!!

*This is delicious with a big side of mashed sweet potato.

Chicken Noodle Soup

I love a big bowl of chicken noodle soup on a good day.

But it sure hits the spot when you are feeling cold and chilly when the winter air hits...

Serves 4-6

10 cups chicken broth (homemade or a gluten free store bought type)

2 cups chopped carrots

2 cups chopped celery

3 cups chopped cooked chicken

3 cups zucchini noodles (you will need a mandolin vegetable spiral machine)

1. Put broth, carrots, celery and chicken in a large soup pot and heat over medium heat until carrots are cooked through.
2. Spoon into bowls and add zucchini noodles and serve.

*For that old home-style feel, serve with some of the Herb Crackers.
*Also makes a nice compliment to the Beef Sliders, or BLT Salad.

Granola "Cereal"

I know cereal is not a meal, even though many of you like to think it is!! ☺
So I added it here for those of you who still enjoy a nice bowl of "cereal" at breakfast.

Preheat oven 350° F

Serves 2

2 cups shredded coconut

2 tbsp. vanilla

¾ cup coconut manna (melted)

4 tsp. honey

1 tbsp. unsweetened applesauce

1. Mix everything together in a large bowl.

2. Spread on parchment lined baking sheet.

3. Bake 15-20 minutes or until golden brown, mix throughout baking process so it does not burn.

*This is one of the most universal recipes. Use it to top baked goods, a parfait filler, morning cereal, ice cream topping or mix with dried fruit (and nuts if you eat them) to make a fun trail mix.

Zucchini Subs

Who does not like a sub filled with all their favorite toppings.
Enjoy this fun twist the clean eating way...

Preheat stove top grill

Serves 2

2 zucchinis

¼ cup olive oil

Deli meat or fresh sliced turkey, chicken or beef, and all the veggie toppings you enjoy!!

1. Slice zucchini length wise into 4 pieces. Discard the "bum" ends.
2. Brush each side of each piece of zucchini with some olive oil and place on hot grill.
3. Grill both sides until tender but not soft.
4. Top one piece of zucchini with your favorite toppings and cover with another piece of zucchini just like you would with a sandwich.

*Other filling options, think tuna or salmon salad.

Lettuce Wraps

Tacos are one of our favorite eat out treats....
So here is an enzyme rich, clean, refreshing, version I came up with. ENJOY!!

Serves 4

2 cup water chestnuts

2 cup mushrooms, chopped

4 green onions, chopped

1 cup celery, chopped

1 cup carrots, chopped

2 cloves fresh garlic, minced

1 tbsp. fresh ginger, grated

2 tbsp. olive oil

Sea salt, to taste

12 lettuce leaves (Boston or Iceberg)

1. In a food processor, add the first 7 ingredients and pulse until chunky.
2. In a wok or large skillet add 2 tbsp. oil and chicken, beef or shrimp, stir fry until done, about 3-5 minutes.
3. Mix the meat and veggie together and scoop 1-2 big spoonfuls of the mixture into each lettuce leave.

*My son likes tomato and olives on his wrap; I personally do not eat tomato as it is a nightshade, his photo turned out way nicer than mine, so we used it!!

Gumbo Soup

I don't know about you.

But at the end of a long day a big hearty bowl of stick to your ribs soup sure sounds good!

Serves 4-6

5 cups chicken broth

1 cup celery, finally chopped

1 cup carrots, finally chopped

1/2 cup onion, finally chopped

1 cup mushrooms, finally chopped

4 cups kale, chopped

1 tbsp. fresh parsley, chopped

Sea salt, dash

6 sausages

1. Add the first 8 ingredients to large pot and cook until veggies are soft.

2. Grill sausage and slice into bite size pieces.

3. Add chopped sausage to soup pot, mix and serve.... :)

*This is a quick, easy and complete meal all on its own. But feel free to play around with the veggies you use to spice things up each time you make it.

Pizzazz Pizza

Need I say more when the word pizza is attached!!

Preheat oven 350° F

Serves 4-6

Crust

1 head cauliflower cooked

2 tbsp chopped chives

1 tbsp chopped parsley

5 cloves garlic pureed (feel free to substitute with roasted garlic)

1/2 cup coconut oil, melted

2 tbsp. olive oil

Toppings

Anything YOU like

1. Add all ingredients to large bowl and mash together until smooth and creamy (you can use a hand blender if you want).
2. Scoop into an 8 or 9 inch spring form pan.
3. Bake 30 minutes or until edges are golden brown.
4. Remove from oven and top with your favorite toppings heat in oven for a few more minutes cut and serve.

*If you are using mushrooms or onions, precook them. I added mushrooms to mine so I steamed them in a pan while the crust was baking.

*This will need to be eaten with a fork as there is no egg to hold the crust together. You can cut into pizza like slices and gently place onto a plate.

*For a thicker crust double the crust recipe. The thicker you make the crust the more it will form and hold together.

Garlic Beef & Asparagus

This is such a flavorful, tasty meal I suggest you make double!!

Preheat grill

Serves 6-8

6-8 sliced pieces of beef

1 lb asparagus

½ cup olive oil

4-5 cloves fresh garlic

1. Steam asparagus until tender but not soft.

2. While asparagus is cooking grill beef until cooked to your liking.

3. In food processor blend olive oil and garlic until creamy.

4. Top each piece of beef with some asparagus and drizzle olive oil cream evenly over each serving.

*Think fish or chicken to mix things up.

Lamb Chops

I think it would be safe to say lamb is one of my son's favorite foods.
So when I ventured into making a fun tasty sauce for this, no one had a chance....

Serves 6

6 lamb chops

Sauce

6 mushrooms

4 tbsp. canned coconut milk

1 tsp. onion flakes

1 tsp. turmeric

Sea salt, dash

1. Grill lamb chops.
2. Toss the other 5 ingredients into food processor and blend until smooth.
3. Put sauce into a sauce pan and heat.
4. Pour evenly over cooked lamb chops.

*This mushroom sauce can be used with any other meat recipe, or as a nice dip, just add more onion flakes and you will have an onion type dip!!

Pancake Perfection

Nothing says Sunday morning like warm pancakes stacked a mile high.

I always make double the batch, freeze them and heat them up for a week day breakfast treat...

Preheat griddle to 400° F

Serves 2-4

1/4 cup coconut flour

2 tbsp. coconut oil (melted)

1 ripe banana

½ cup blueberries (fresh or frozen)

1/4 cup canned coconut milk + 1 tbsp.

1 tbsp. gluten free vanilla

1/4 tsp. apple pie spice

1. Toss everything except the blueberries into blender and blend until smooth. Add in blueberries and mix by hand.
2. Pour batter onto griddle into silver dollar size pancakes.
3. Grill until golden brown.
4. Top with additional coconut oil and drizzle with pure maple syrup (if you want!!)........ ENJOY.

*Switch up the blueberries for peaches, pears or any other fresh diced fruit.

Beef Burger Sliders

These are super quick and easy for those nights when you are rushing out the door ....
Add to a huge side salad or steamed veggies and you have a Magnificent Meal!!

Preheat grill (stove top or BBQ)

Serves 4-6

1 pound ground beef

1/2 cup chopped onions

1 tbsp. garlic powder

1 tbsp. crushed rosemary

1 tbsp. mint (optional)

1 tbsp. raw honey

1/2 cup chopped chives

1. With hands mix everything together in bowl.
2. Make into slider size patties.
3. Grill on stove top or BBQ.

*These can be made with ground chicken or turkey too. They will be more delicate though so be gentle with them!!

Fennel Chops

Add a little summer flair to your winter meal with this bright refreshing recipe.

Pre heat grill

Serves 4-6

6 large pork chops (deboned is fine)

1 fresh fennel bulb, chopped

½ watermelon, diced

1 mango, peeled and pitted (optional)

2-3 tbsp. olive oil

2 limes, juiced

Fresh mint, to taste

Sea salt, dash

1. Grill pork chops, when cooked put on separate plate.
2. Add the fennel and olive oil to the grill and cook 10-15 minutes.
3. Mix cooked fennel, lime juice, dash of sea salt, watermelon, mint and mango (if you chose to use it) in a large bowl.
4. Put fennel mixture over the grilled pork chops, and away you go!!

*Feel free to play around with the fruit; try melon, peaches or mango.

Chicken Samosas

My husband loves samosas; these are a lighter baked version.

Preheat oven 350° F

Serves 2

Filling

1 cup chicken, precooked

1 cup sweet potato, cooked and peeled

Crust

1/3 cup coconut flour

¼ cup water

1/3 cup coconut oil (melted)

½ tsp. cinnamon

¼ cup maple syrup

1 tsp. lemon juice

½ tsp. garlic powder

½ tsp. ginger powder

½ tsp. sage (optional)

1 tsp. parsley

½ tsp. turmeric

½ tsp. cinnamon

1 tsp. onion powder

Sauce

¼ cup honey, melted

2 tbsp. dijon mustard

1. Mix everything together in a bowl except filling and sauce ingredients.

2. When it forms into a dough, take little handful amounts and pat down to a patty like shape (see attached photo).

3. Place on parchment lined baking sheet and bake 20 minutes or until browned.

4. Mix chicken and sweet potato together.

5. Mix honey and mustard together in small bowl.

6. Take cooked patties and fill with potato mixture and top with another patty.

7. Drizzle with honey dijon sauce.

*Change things up by subbing the chicken for diced beef or salmon.

Tasty Treats

Strawberry Custard Cups

This was inspired by my daughter's favorite banana strawberry smoothie....

Preheat oven 350° F

Makes 4 tarts

Crust

½ cup shredded coconut

3 tbsp. apple sauce

3 dates (pitted & soaked)

½ tsp. vanilla

Filling

3 large strawberries

½ banana, chilled not frozen

2 tbsp. coconut manna

1. Place all crust ingredients in food processor and blend.

2. Evenly divide coconut mixture into muffin pan.

3. Bake 20–30 minutes or until golden brown.

4. While crust is baking puree strawberries, banana and coconut manna together.

5. Once shells are cooled fill with strawberry filling and enjoy.

*Make your taste buds sing each time, by using other berries or soft fruit in place of the strawberries.

Apple Pie

Apple pie is one of those original classics that never die.
Here is a healthy high fiber twist on an old time favorite...

Preheat oven 350° F

Serves 6-8

Crust

4 sweet potatoes

2 tsp. cinnamon

1 tsp. vanilla

½ cup shredded coconut

4 dates (pitted & soaked)

Filling

2 apples of choice

½ cup apple juice

1 tbsp. maple syrup

1 tsp. apple pie spice

1. Put all crust ingredients in a food processor and blend until creamy.
2. Fill a 9" spring form pan and bake until sides are golden brown approximately 40-50 minutes.
3. While crust is baking put all filling ingredients in a sauce pan and boil for 5 minutes, remove from heat and let sit.
4. Once crust has cooled pour apple mixture over crust and enjoy.

*You can also turn this into an apple pumpkin pudding, by eliminating the baking process and simply mixing everything together in the food processor and serving in a lovely pudding cup.

Mango ice cream

This dairy free sugar free version is a great topping for the Apple Pie recipe.
Or topped with our clean eating version of Granola.....

Serves 2

1 whole ripe banana (frozen)

1 cup frozen mango

½ canned coconut milk

1. Put everything in a high speed blender and puree until smooth and creamy.

2. Scoop into a container and freeze until ready to use.

*Make this into a yummy smoothie by simply adding more coconut milk until it is the creaminess you like. Pour into a big mug and sip away!!

Raspberry Parfait

This parfait is pretty enough to be the finishing touch to the end of a lovely dinner party. Or as a healthy treat to yourself after a long week!!

Serves 2

Granola Topping

2 cups shredded coconut

2 tbsp. vanilla

¾ cup coconut manna (melted)

4 tsp. honey

1 tbsp. unsweetened applesauce

1. Mix everything together in a large bowl.
2. Spread on parchment lined baking sheet.
3. Bake until golden brown 15-20 minutes.
4. Mix throughout baking process so it does not burn.

Filling

1 ripe banana

1 cup fresh raspberries

1. Layer the granola and the raspberry filling

*Feel free to substitute the raspberries for any other soft fruit of your choice.

Hot Cocoa

Hot cocoa is one of the best drinks to snuggle up with on a cold winter day.
This version is sure to fill your tummy!!

Serves 2

1 ripe banana

1/2 tbsp. vanilla

1 tsp. cinnamon

¼ tsp. nutmeg

1 tbsp. unsweetened cocoa powder

4 dates (pitted & soaked)

1 cup coconut milk (canned will make it thicker, but regular is fine too)

1 cup apple juice

1. Put all the ingredients in a blender and puree until smooth and creamy.

*You can heat this up, or drink it cold like a thick milkshake.
*Eliminate the coconut milk and once pureed, scoop into contain and freeze into chocolate ice cream.

Grilled Pears

Pears are full of so much natural fiber and are one of nature's sweet treats.
This dessert is not only good for you it tastes great too!!

Preheat grill

Serves 4

2 pears

8 dates (pitted & soaked)

1 lemon juiced

1. Slice pears horizontally in half and remove the core.

2. Place sliced side down on grill and grill until browned.

3. Put dates and lemon juice in food processor and pulse until blended.

4. Pour date sauce over pears.

*Substitute the pears with fresh pineapple slices or fresh peaches.

"Rice" Pudding

Don't know about you, but one of my all-time favorite cold weather treats is rice pudding. Here is a great grain free alternative...

Serves 2

2 cups coconut flakes, large not shredded

1 cup canned coconut milk

1/2 cup water

2 tbsp. pure maple syrup

1 tbsp. cinnamon

1/4 cup raisins (optional)

1/4 cup dried apricots chopped (optional)

1. Combine everything in a stove top pan.
2. Cook over medium heat 10 minutes or until thick...
3. That's it!! Can you say YUM!!

Cinnamon Cookies

These have a nice warming factor with the hint of cinnamon.
Yet has a nice sweetness from the coconut sugar.

Preheat oven 350° F

Makes 4 cookies (other cookie cutter shapes may make more cookies)

Dough

1/3 cup coconut oil, melted

¼ cup water

1/3 cup coconut flour

½ tsp. cinnamon

¼ cup maple syrup

Icing

¼ cup coconut sugar

2 tbsp. cinnamon

2 tbsp. coconut oil, melted

1. Put all ingredients into a large bowl and mix until forms dough.
2. Put dough onto a parchment lined baking sheet and top with another piece of parchment paper.
3. Roll dough out (not too thin) and with cookie cutter cut into shapes.
4. Mix icing ingredients.
5. Bake 20-25 minutes or until golden brown and frost with icing.

*These cookies can be frosted or eaten plain.
*For a plain unfrosted but flavored cookie, add a drop of your favorite extract to the mix.

Black Cherry Ice Cream

Not only does this have a fabulous rich color,
It goes great as a topping on any of our pie or cookie recipes.

Serves 2

1 whole ripe banana, frozen

1 cup black cherries, frozen

¼ cup canned coconut milk

1. Put everything into a high-speed blender and puree until creamy and smooth.

2. Scoop into container and freeze until needed.

*To make this a fun and tasty milkshake add about ½-1 cup coconut milk and blend until smooth...ENJOY!!

*For a summer treat, freeze into fun popsicle shapes.

Peppermint Fudge!!

Fudge kind of falls into the pizza category.
There are no other words needed when we hear the word FUDGE!!

Makes 12 mini cups

½ cup coconut manna

1 tbsp. unsweetened cocoa

1 tbsp. maple syrup

½ cup canned coconut milk

½ tsp. peppermint extract (optional)

1. Put all into food processor and puree.
2. Line a 12 serving mini muffin tin with paper liners and fill evenly with mixture.
3. Put into the freezer and freeze until firm.
4. Let stand 5 minutes before serving so they will lift out of the tins easily.

*Don't like peppermint, add any other extract flavor of your choice or leave plain.

Lemon Macaroons

These are grain, gluten, egg, sugar, soy, nut and dairy free, but definitely not taste free.
They pack a pleasant little punch with the lemon!!

Preheat oven 350° F

Makes 16 cookies

1 cup unsweetened shredded coconut

4 dates (pitted & soaked)

4 tbsp. melted coconut manna

1/2 lemon, juiced

1 tsp. lemon zest

4 tbsp. coconut milk

1. Add everything to a food processor and puree until blended.
2. Scoop large teaspoon size amounts onto a parchment lined baking sheet.
3. Bake 15 minutes or until golden brown.

Bursting Berry Pie...

I asked my kiddies what I should call this pie and they said "I want more pie" they loved it...
So this is definitely two thumbs up kid approved!!

Preheat oven 350° F

Serves 4-6

CRUST

2 cups shredded coconut

1/2 cup unsweetened applesauce

3 dates (pitted & soaked))

FILLING

1 bag frozen mixed berries

6 dried figs (soaked until soft, and save the water they were soaked in)

1. In a food processor add coconut, applesauce and dates.

2. Blend until a dough like consistency.

3. Line a spring form pan with parchment paper and fill with coconut batter.

4. Press down to form a crust like shape.

5. Bake 20 minutes or until golden brown.

6. Blend soaked figs and a little of the fig water in the food processor.

7. Blend and add water as needed until you get a jam like consistency.

8. Add berries to a stove top pan and heat until softened, add in fig puree and mix together.

9. Cook a few more minutes and pour over crust.

ENJOY!!

*Have some fun switching things up by using whichever fruit is in season.

Rum Raisin Apples

These are like a Caramel Candy Apple in a bowl!!

Serves 2

2 red apples of choice

2 tbsp. coconut cream (not oil)

¼ cup maple syrup

¼ cup raisins

1. In sauce pan bring coconut cream, maple syrup and raisins to a boil over low heat.
2. Remove from heat as soon as it boils and let stand about 10 minutes.
3. While sauce is sitting spiral the apples, it is easiest with a veggie spiral machine (you can pick one up on line for about $25).
4. Put apple strings into serving cups, give the sauce a stir, top apples with sauce.

*For a little spunk add a drop or two of rum extract, or if you'd like, the real thing!!

Peppermint Thins

I love chocolate and peppermint, think Junior Mints & Peppermint Patties
(Oh, and Easter cream eggs, but that's a story for another day)

Makes approx. 8-10 squares

1/3 cup shredded coconut

2 tbsp. coconut oil (melted)

2 tsp. peppermint extract

1 tbsp. coconut flour

1 tbsp. coconut manna

Chocolate Coating

1/3 cup enjoy-life chocolate chips

1/2 tbsp. coconut oil

1. Mix first 5 ingredients together in a bowl and spread onto cookie sheet and freeze until hard.

2. While the coconut mixture is in the freezer melt the chocolate chips and coconut oil in the microwave, mix and set aside.

3. Remove coconut mix from freezer, let sit a few minutes and cut into bite size squares (I used a pizza cutter to cut them).

4. Dip coconut pieces into melted chocolate and put in fridge until chocolate sets.

*Change up the flavors by replacing the peppermint with other extracts.

Peach Pie

This pie is PERFECTION!!

I am not sure what is better, the aroma through the kitchen as this pie is baking, or the taste when you are eating it....

Preheat oven 350° F

Serves 6

Dough

3/4 cup coconut oil (melted)

1/2 cup water

¾ cup coconut flour

1 1/2 tsp. cinnamon

1 tsp. dried orange peel spice

½ cup pure maple syrup

Filling

1-14 oz. can of sliced peaches in water (reserve juice from the can and 3 peach slices)

Topping

4 dates (pitted & soaked) (plus 3 reserved peaches and juice from above)

1. Put first 6 ingredients in large mixing bowl and combine by hand until all mixed.
2. Put dough into a 9" spring form pan and spread out.
3. Layer the sliced peaches around the crust.
4. Add reserved peach juice, the 3 peaches you saved, 4 dates and puree until smooth.
5. Spread over the peaches and crust.
6. Bake 40 minutes or until crust has browned around the edges.

*For a pineapple upsides down version use pineapples and for a nice fall treat use pears.

Candy Apple Pops

Nothing is sure to trigger childhood memories like a Candy Apple.
BUT, they are definitely not a clean eating food.
That's OK, these ones are wayyyy tasty, and a little goes a long way!!!

Makes 8

1 cup shredded coconut unsweetened

1/4 cup dried unsweetened cranberries

1 tsp. pure vanilla

3/4 cup coconut manna

2 tbsp. apple sauce

2 dates (pitted & soaked)

4 heaping tsp. raw honey

8 mini muffin wrappers

1. Toss everything but the honey in a food processor and mix.
2. Scoop out mixture and roll into small balls and place in muffin wrappers.
3. Insert sticks and place on a plate.
4. In small sauce pan heat the honey on very low until turns golden brown.
5. Pour over the "apple" balls and put in freezer until set....

*These can be turned into pretty little squares, simply spread mixture into a square baking pan instead of rolling into balls, and follow remaining directions.
*For a special holiday treat drizzle with a tiny bit of melted dairy free chocolate.

"Granola" Bars

These are great grab and go energy picker uppers.

Makes 6-8 bars

Granola

2 cups shredded coconut

2 tbsp. vanilla

¾ cup coconut manna (melted)

4 tsp. honey

1 tbsp. unsweetened applesauce

1. Mix everything together in a large bowl and spread on parchment lined baking sheet.

2. Bake 15-20 minutes or until golden brown. Mix throughout baking process so it does not burn.

Fillings

1 cup unsweetened dried blueberries

1 cup chopped dried apples

¾ cup honey, melted

1 cup dried unsweetened cranberries

¼ tsp. apple pie spice

1 tbsp. coconut oil (melted)

1. Put everything including the granola, in a large bowl and toss with your hands until all mixed and coated with the honey.

2. Scoop into a glass pan and spread out.

3. Place in freezer for 30 minutes, remove and slice into bar shapes. They will still be a little delicate so be careful when moving them around.

4. Wrap in individual pieces and return to freezer to set longer.

5. Keep stored in freezer until ready to eat.

*If you leave the bars in the freezer too long before cutting into shapes, they won't cut as they will get too hard.
*Play around with the spices and fruits for a different taste.

131

Choconana Drops

This is like a bite size piece of banana cake.

It is super moist and will satisfy that craving for a little taste of chocolate.

Preheat oven 350° F

Makes approx. 20 cookies

2 ripe bananas mashed

1 tbsp. coconut oil

1 cup canned coconut milk

1 tbsp. water

¾ cup coconut flour (you may need to add a little more depending on the brand of coconut flour you use. If so just add 1 tbsp. at a time until it is like cookie batter)

2 tbsp. honey

½ cup chocolate chips (I use the Enjoy life brand they are gluten, dairy, egg and soy free)

1. Put all ingredients in a large bowl and mix by hand.
2. Put tbsp. size drops on a parchment lined cookie sheet.
3. Bake 30-40 minutes or until golden brown.

*These are very soft and chewy cookies, so keep them stored in the fridge for freshness.

Flourless Cookies

Don't like coconut flour? These will hit the spot for sure.

Feel free to play around with the spices and fruits to create your own favorite soft chew!!

Preheat 350° F

Makes 12 cookies

1 ripe banana

1 sweet potato baked and skin removed

1 tsp. vanilla

¼ cup raisins

½ cup apple pieces (dried or fresh)

½ tsp. apple pie spice

3 tbsp. maple syrup (optional)

1. Mash everything together in a large bowl until banana and sweet potato are completely mashed.

2. Spoon tablespoon size dough onto parchment lined cookie sheet and flatten with fork.

3. Bake 30 minutes or until cookies are cooked through and bottom of cookie is brown.

*These can be eaten raw. Simply shape into cookie shape and serve with a fork.

"S'mores"

I was staring down some left over cookie dough one day, when this idea popped into my head. These are fun and easy, yet sure to impress any hostess or guest.

Preheat oven 350° F

Makes 12 cookies

Dough

1/3 cup coconut oil (melted)

¼ cup water

1/3 cup coconut flour + 1 tbsp.

½ tsp. cinnamon

¼ cup maple syrup

White drizzle

2 tbsp. coconut manna

1 tbsp. coconut oil (melted)

Dark drizzle

2 tbsp. chocolate chips (I used Enjoy life; they are gluten, dairy, egg and soy free)

1 tbsp. coconut oil

1. Mix everything in large bowl until it forms dough.
2. Roll into balls and bake 20 minutes or until golden brown.
3. Once cookies are baked melt dark drizzle ingredients together and mix.
4. Mix white drizzle ingredients together, no need to melt.
5. Pour drizzle over the cookies and be ready to drool. Say that 10 times!!

Sticky Buns

There is nothing better than eating a meal and getting to lick all the goodness off your fingers.

Think ribs and chicken wings.

And ok yes, apparently I did not go to etiquette class!!

Preheat oven 350

Makes about 8 mini muffins

1/3 cup coconut oil (melted)

1 tbsp. vanilla, gluten free

1/3 tsp. baking powder

1/4 cup maple syrup

1/3 cup + 2 tbsp. coconut flour

"Caramel" Sauce

1 tbsp. coconut oil

2 tbsp. maple syrup

1. Line mini muffin tin.
2. Add the first 4 ingredients into a large mixing bowl and blend with hand mixer.
3. Slowly add flour and continue to mix.
4. Scoop a large teaspoon of dough into the lined muffin tins, or until about half filled.
5. Bake 20 minutes or until golden brown and a tooth pick comes out clean.
6. Let cool, while cooling add caramel sauce ingredients to a small sauce pan over high heat and continue stirring until the sauce comes to a full boil.
7. Take off stove and evenly distribute over each mini muffin.
8. Put muffins into freezer and let freeze until the "caramel" gets hard.

*Let the muffins sit out for a few minutes when you are ready to eat them so they slightly soften and you are able to pull the wrapper off, and don't break a tooth!!!

Smashing Smoothies, Juices & Dressings

Greentini

This is a clean eating spin on an Appletini and Melon Margarita combined.

Serves 2

¼ cup grapefruit juice (fresh squeezed if possible)

¼ of a lime, juiced

½ honey dew melon (flesh only)

1. Toss everything into a high-speed blender and puree until smooth and frothy.

2. Serve over ice.

*If you want to kick up your heels a little, add a dibble of your favorite "shot" to it ;)

Waterberry Smoothie

Super nourishing, hydrating and refreshing!!

Serves 2

1/2 of a 1/2 of watermelon (catch that!!) ¼ of a watermelon

15 strawberries

1/2 lime, juiced

1. Toss everything into a blender and Enjoy!!

"Pink" Lemonade Juice

This has a real immune boosting, picker upper, eye opening freshness to it...
Enjoy it as a start to your day, when you are feeling a little dehydrated or just cause!

Serves 1 large glass or 2 small glasses

2 heads romaine lettuce

1 whole lemon, peeled

1 large granny smith apple

1 large beet (raw)

1" ginger (optional, the ginger will add warmth to the juice)

1. Juice everything in juicer and chug-a-lug!!

*To make this a complete green juice, leave out the beet and it will be pure green goodness!!

Holiday Coconut Milk...Pumpkin Spice

After seeing all the holiday flavored "milks" hitting the markets, I sat in frustration as my kids were asking me to please buy some...

Yes they were gluten free, dairy free, egg free, but did you ever take notice to what they were NOT free of!! Yuck...

So I muddled through the market thinking how I could recreate these "milks" so my kids did not feel deprived.

We love Pumpkin, so the first one that came to mind was this one...

Serves 2 small servings

1 cup coconut milk (canned or regular)

1/2 cup pumpkin puree

1/2 cup water from soaked dates

1 tsp. vanilla gluten free

2 dates (pitted & soaked)

½ tsp. each of nutmeg, cinnamon, and pumpkin pie spice (feel free to adjust spices to your liking)

1. Put all in a blender and blend until super smooth and blended.

VEGGIE SMOOTHIE

*Give this a try when you are in a hurry and need a quick grab and go,
highly nutritious, vitamin packed, filler-up-r!!*

Serves 1 large cup or 2 small

1 banana

2 large carrots

2 handfuls of spinach or kale

1/2 cup blueberries

6 strawberries

1/2 cup coconut milk (canned or regular)

½ cup to 1 cup water (depends how thick you want it)

1. Toss all into high speed blender like a vita-mix and pulse until smooth!!

Kiwi "Kooler" Smoothie

This has such a nice refreshing flavor, perfect for a warm summer's day.

Makes 1 large glass or 2 small

1 cup coconut milk (canned or regular)

1 bartlett pear

2 kiwis, peeled

1 lime, juiced

Cinnamon, just a dash

1. Toss everything into blender, kick back and chill!!

Dressings

Mix, match & play with the ingredients from these dressings

But make sure you have fun!!

Orange Blossom

1/2 cup orange juice

2 tbsp. fresh lemon juice

1/3 cup olive oil

1 clove garlic, grated

1 tbsp. chopped fresh parsley

1. Whisk all together and ENJOY!!

Magnificent Mustard Dressing

2 tbsp. olive oil

2 tbsp. fresh chopped herbs such as chives, parsley, thyme, mint, basil

1/2 tsp. lemon juice

1/2 tbsp. dried mustard or dijon

1. Whisk all together and say "YUM"!!

Blasting Blueberry Dressing

1/2 cup blueberries

1/4 cup olive oil

1" fresh ginger

1 lime, juiced

1. Toss all ingredients into a blender, blend until smooth, and pour over salad greens and mix.

Honey and Spice Dressing

1/4 cup olive oil

3 tbsp. raw honey

2 tbsp. dijon mustard

1. Whisk first three ingredients together, mix with greens and top with a splash of balsamic vinegar.

Recipe Index